D0916820

Recipe for
DISASTER
The Science of **Foodborne Illness**

HEADLINE SCIENCE

by Darlene R. Stille

Content Adviser:
John M. Lammert, Ph.D., Professor,
Department of Biology, Gustavus Adolphus College

Science Adviser:
Terrence E. Young Jr., M.Ed., M.L.S.,
Jefferson Parish (Louisiana) Public School System

COMPASS POINT BOOKS
a capstone imprint

Reading Adviser:
Alexa L. Sandmann, Ed.D., Professor of Literacy,
College and Graduate School of Education, Health,
and Human Services, Kent State University

Compass Point Books • 151 Good Counsel Drive, P. O. Box 669 • Mankato, MN 56002-0669

This book was manufactured with paper containing
at least 10 percent post-consumer waste.

Library of Congress Cataloging-in-Publication Data
Stille, Darlene R.
  Recipe for disaster : the science of foodborne illness /
by Darlene R. Stille.
    p. cm. — (Headline science)
  Includes bibliographical references and index.
  ISBN 978-0-7565-4216-0 (library binding)
  1. Foodborne diseases—Juvenile literature. I. Title. II. Series.
  RA601.5.S75 2010
  615.9'54—dc22   2009034851

Editor: Jennifer Fretland VanVoorst
Designer: Ted Williams
Media Researcher: Svetlana Zhurkin
Production Specialist: Jane Klenk

Photographs ©: AP Photo/Bebeto Matthews, 39; AP Photo/Jaime Puebla, 20; AP Photo/Kevork Djansezian, 38;
AP Photo/Nati Harnik, 18; AP Photo/Paul Sakuma, 29; CDC, 13, 15; CDC/Janice Haney Carr, 10, 16, 33, 37; Corbis/
Royalty-free, 7; Dreamstime/Pavel Losevsky, 28; FDA/Black Star/Michael Falco, 25, 26, 27; Getty Images/China
Photos, 5; Getty Images/David Silverman, 19; iStockphoto/Christine Glade, 32; iStockphoto/MBPhoto, 34, cover;
iStockphoto/Morgan Lane Photography, 12, cover; iStockphoto/Naomi Bassitt, 8; iStockphoto/Rob Belknap, 22;
iStockphoto/Ron Sumners, 11; iStockphoto/Slobo Mitic, 42; iStockphoto/Stefanie Timmermann, 41; Peter Arnold/
Medicimage/The Medical File, 35; Shutterstock/Cathleen Clapper, 24; Shutterstock/Cenorman, 30, cover; Shut-
terstock/Ferencz Teglas, 40; Shutterstock/Sebastian Kaulitzki, cover; Shutterstock/VR Photos, 21.

Visit Compass Point Books on the Internet at *www.compasspointbooks.com*
or e-mail your request to *custserv@compasspointbooks.com*

Chapter 1
Poison on Your Plate

Page 4

Chapter 3
Handle With Care

Page 17

Chapter 5
Treating the Toxins

Page 31

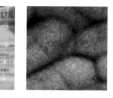

Chapter 2
Attack of the Germs

Page 9

Chapter 4
Disease Detectives

Page 23

Chapter 6
An Ounce of Prevention

Page 36

Timeline	Page 44
Glossary	Page 45
Further Resources	Page 46
Source Notes	Page 47
Index	Page 48

INDIA BANS CHOCOLATE IMPORTS FROM CHINA

The China Post
July 28, 2009

India has banned imports of chocolates and chocolate products from China due to fears they might be contaminated with the industrial chemical melamine. India prohibited imports of Chinese milk and milk products last September ... [after] more than 20 Chinese dairy makers were found ... to have been selling melamine-tainted milk products that caused the deaths of six infants in China and sickened nearly 300,000. Melamine is a chemical normally used to make plastics but it emerged that it had been routinely mixed into Chinese milk and dairy products to give them the impression of having higher protein content. The scandal quickly became a global problem, with Chinese dairy products around the world recalled or banned after they were found to be tainted with the chemical.

Problems with food in one country can rapidly become worldwide concerns. In China in the summer of 2008, parents noticed that something was making their babies sick. That something was a chemical called melamine. It is usually used to make plastics and fertilizer. But Chinese dairy companies had added melamine to milk to cover up the fact that they had watered down the milk to make more money.

In quality tests, melamine can make a food appear to have more protein than it does.

Melamine can cause kidney stones and even kidney failure. The bodies of healthy adults and older children could cope with what they drank. The small bodies of babies, however, were less able to cope. And milk was the babies' main food. Nearly 300,000 Chinese babies in 2008 became sick

Melamine, an industrial chemical, increased the apparent protein content of baby formula, but it killed six babies and sickened hundreds of thousands of others.

KEEPING CURRENT

News changes every minute, and readers need access to the latest information to keep current. Here are a few key search terms to help you locate up-to-the-minute foodborne illness headlines:

botulism

Centers for Disease Control and Prevention (CDC)

Escherichia coli (E. coli)

Food and Drug Administration (FDA)

food recalls

melamine

irradiation

Salmonella

NOW YOU KNOW

The U.S. government recalled 60 million packages of dog and cat food in 2007 after about 14,000 pets became ill and 16 died. Investigators found that a wheat ingredient that U.S. pet food makers had imported from China contained the industrial chemical melamine.

after drinking the poisoned milk, and six died.

IS IT SAFE?

How safe is our food supply? This is a question that people all over the world are asking. People worry about contamination by chemicals used on farmland to kill pests or weeds. They worry about chemicals fed to animals to make them grow bigger and faster. They worry about chemicals that get into food accidentally. When indus-

Chemicals sprayed from airplanes protect crops by killing pests, but they introduce toxins into the environment, which can harm human health.

trial chemicals, such as mercury and PCBs, are dumped into oceans, lakes, and rivers, they build up in fish. Mercury can damage the human nervous system. PCBs harm various organs and may cause cancer. Researchers in the United Kingdom found evidence that some food colorings and chemicals used to preserve food may cause children to become hyperactive.

Chemicals are a serious threat. The greatest danger to our food supply, however, comes from tiny organisms that can only be seen with microscopes. Have you ever had stomach flu or food poisoning? People use these terms when they experience nausea, vomiting, intestinal cramps, diarrhea,

Almost any type of food can contain toxins that cause foodborne illness.

and sometimes headache and fever. Doctors call these symptoms gastroenteritis, which means an inflammation of the stomach and intestines.

Outbreaks of gastroenteritis can occur in places where many people are together, such as hospitals, schools, resorts, restaurants, and cruise ships. But gastroenteritis also occurs among people who seem to have no connection with one another. A big outbreak might even occur at about the same time among people who live in different states.

What do all of these sick people have in common? They all ate food or drank beverages contaminated with microorganisms that cause gastroenteritis. Even though the symptoms they cause are much the same, a wide variety of microorganisms can contaminate food. The food can contain bacteria, viruses, or parasites. In addition, some microorganisms give off a toxin, a poisonous substance that can make people very sick. Medical scientists call the sicknesses caused by anything in or on the things we eat or drink foodborne illness.

"NOROVIRUS" CRUISE CANCELLED

>>> Telegraph.co.uk
July 8, 2009

The *Marco Polo*, a ship at the center of a suspected norovirus outbreak, is to cut short its voyage ... its operators said last night. Hundreds of passengers and crew on the ship ... have shown symptoms of norovirus and are being treated on board. ... About 380 people on board the ship are showing symptoms of the illness. ... The norovirus is also called the "winter vomiting disease" because people usually get it during the winter months, but it can occur at any time of the year. It spreads very easily from person to person and can survive for several days in a contaminated area. The bug can also spread through contact with surfaces or objects that are contaminated, or by eating contaminated food or water.

Any kind of beverage or food—vegetables, beef, poultry, and fish—can become contaminated with disease-causing microorganisms. Scientists have found that microorganisms cause more than 250 types of foodborne illnesses. Bacteria, however, are the most common culprits.

Scientists using powerful microscopes can see bacteria. They are single-celled organisms, but they are not plants or animals. Bacteria are in a kingdom by themselves. They come in three basic shapes—thin and long like rods or capsules, round like balls, and twisted like corkscrews.

When people eat disease-causing bacteria, the germs head right for their intestines. The bacteria attach themselves to the walls of the intestines. They reproduce by dividing in half over and over again. Sometimes it only takes a few hours for enough bacteria to grow to cause sickness. Sometimes it takes several days. Vomiting and diarrhea occur as the body tries to get rid of the harmful bacteria.

Seen under an electron microscope, Escherichia coli bacteria look like capsules or sausages.

Gastroenteritis can lead to cramps, vomiting, and diarrhea, as the body tries to rid itself of harmful bacteria.

These are some bacteria that can make us sick:

• *Escherichia coli.* Not all bacteria cause disease. In fact, most of the billions of bacteria you come in contact with are harmless. Some are even helpful. The *Escherichia coli* bacterium, for example, lives in the intestines of humans, cattle, and other mammals. E. coli has many forms, which scientists call strains. The strain called E. coli O157:H7 is the one that usually causes outbreaks of foodborne illness in North America. All E. coli bacteria look the same. They are shaped like thin rods or capsules. Only an expert can tell the difference between helpful and harmful strains. In addition to cramps, vomiting, and diarrhea, the E. coli O157:H7 strain can cause kidney failure and death.

• *Salmonella.* Another well-known group of bacteria that cause foodborne illness is *Salmonella.* Strains of these bacteria live in the intestines of chickens and other birds, lizards, turtles, and cattle and other mammals. *Salmonella* bacteria can sometimes be found in uncooked eggs. This bacterium causes vomiting, diarrhea, and fever. In people who are weakened by some other illness, *Salmonella* can get into the bloodstream. When this occurs, the infection can cause death. One type, *Salmonella typhi*, causes typhoid fever. *Salmonella typhi* in city water supplies once caused major outbreaks of typhoid fever in the United States and Europe.

• *Listeria.* Bacteria in the *Listeria* group can cause serious illness in sick or elderly people. In pregnant women, *Listeria* can harm their unborn children. People infected with the *Listeria* bacterium develop muscle aches, fever,

Most any kind of food can, under the right conditions, become host to bacteria that cause illness.

diarrhea, and vomiting. Sometimes the germs attack the nervous system.

• *Campylobacter.* The U.S. Centers for Disease Control and Prevention reports that *Campylobacter* causes most cases of diarrhea throughout the world. These bacteria live in the intestines of birds, including chickens and turkeys. *Campylobacter*, along with E. coli and *Salmonella*, can spoil a trip with an illness called traveler's diarrhea. This foodborne illness strikes many people who travel to developing countries in Africa, Asia, the Middle East, and Latin America.

• *Shigella*. Another group of bacteria that can cause gastroenteritis is *Shigella*. As with other foodborne illnesses, the vomiting and diarrhea caused by *Shigella* can lead to dehydration, which can be dangerous and sometimes deadly. Dehydration is a condition in which the body loses too much fluid.

• *Vibrio*. Some of the most dangerous bacteria belong to the *Vibrio* group. Some *Vibrio* live in freshwater, and others live in seawater. One type of *Vibrio* causes cholera, an often deadly disease. Cholera causes gastroenteritis and severe diarrhea, which leads to leg cramps and dehydration.

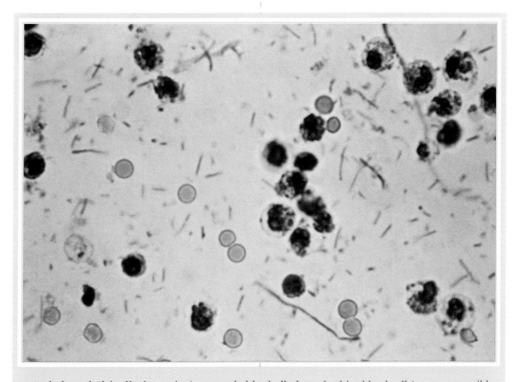

Rod-shaped Shigella *bacteria (surrounded by ball-shaped white blood cells) are responsible for dystentery, a disease common in places with overcrowding and poor sanitation.*

VIRUSES IN FOOD

Viruses cause many kinds of diseases, from AIDS to the common cold. Only a few types of viruses cause foodborne illnesses. But many kinds of food can carry these viruses.

Viruses are so small that scientists can see them only under the most powerful microscopes, called electron microscopes. Viruses are strange organisms. They are not really alive, but they are not dead either. A virus is just a package of genes wrapped in a protein coat. The genes contain a blueprint for making more viruses. Unlike plants, animals, bacteria, and other organisms, viruses do not contain the kind of molecules needed to put more viruses together. Instead, when viruses invade cells, their genes command the cells to produce more viruses.

The symptoms caused by a foodborne virus depend on what kind of cell it invades. Noroviruses invade intestinal cells, causing vomiting and diarrhea. Noroviruses are often responsible for outbreaks of illness aboard cruise ships and in restaurants,

school cafeterias, and hospitals. Noroviruses are very contagious. Scientists do not think these viruses live in animals, as E. coli and other bacteria do. Instead they pass from one infected person to another.

Another kind of virus, the hepatitis A virus, attacks cells in the liver. It causes a liver disease called hepatitis A. Hepatitis A infection causes fever, upset stomach, and a tired feeling. The skin of a person with hepatitis may have a yellowish color. This condition is called jaundice.

PARASITES AND NATURAL POISONS

The parasites *Giardia* and *Cryptosporidium* can contaminate food. People can also become infected by drinking unsanitary water or swimming in lakes or rivers containing these parasites. The parasites live in the intestines and reproduce by laying eggs. They eat the nutrients in cells. Sometimes they cause vomiting and diarrhea, but sometimes the infected person does not know the parasites are there at all.

Some bacteria, including E. coli O157:H7, give off toxins. The bacte-

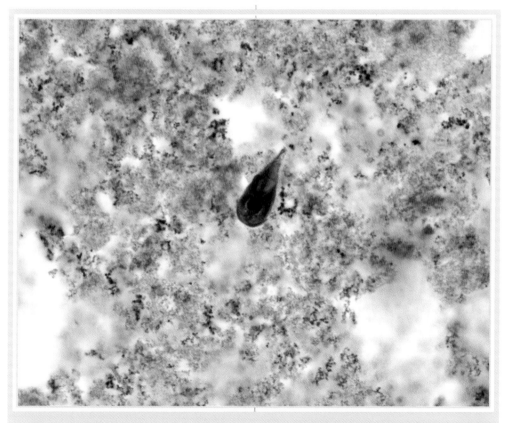

Giardia is a microscopic, teardrop-shaped, one-celled parasite that lodges in a host's intestines and can cause diarrhea and other digestive discomforts.

rium *Clostridium botulinum* gives off the botulin toxin. Botulin causes a foodborne illness called botulism. The botulin toxin attacks the nervous system and causes paralysis. Foodborne botulism can occur after a person eats food that has not been properly canned, especially home-canned food.

Staphylococcus aureus is another bacterium that produces a toxin. It normally infects the skin. But the CDC estimates that this bacterium causes about 185,000 cases of foodborne illness in the United States every year. The toxin causes gastroenteritis.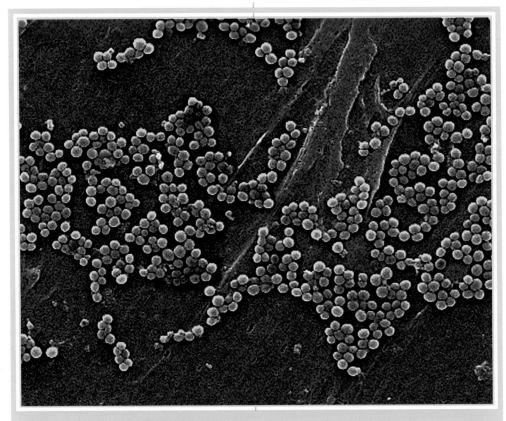

Some varieties of Staphylococcus aureus *are resistant to antibiotics; they are known as "superbugs."*

SALMONELLA CASES SPUR FRESNO GROUND BEEF RECALL

The San Francisco Chronicle
August 7, 2009

More than 800,000 pounds of ground beef from a Fresno (California) processing plant have been recalled because of concerns the meat might be linked to a *Salmonella* outbreak, federal officials said Thursday. ... The U.S. Department of Agriculture's Food and Safety Inspection Service is investigating the outbreak. So far, 40 people in nine states ... have been sickened, according to the California Department of Public Health. At least four people have been hospitalized. All are expected to recover. ... The ground beef recall is the second major recall from *Salmonella* contamination this year. In January, a *Salmonella* outbreak that sickened about 500 people and killed at least nine was linked to peanut butter and led to a major recall of dozens of products.

Many bacteria, such as *Salmonella*, *Listeria*, and E. coli, normally live in the intestines of cattle, chicken, turkey, and other animals raised for their meat. The animals are not sick. During processing, however, what is in their intestines sometimes spills out. With the intestinal contents come the bacteria.

Meat processing plants in the United States have ways to keep the bacteria away from the meat. Workers clean floors, tools, and tables regularly. They wash the carcasses of the dead animals. They use chemicals that kill germs. Government inspectors visit the meatpacking plants to be sure the plants obey food safety rules.

Sometimes, however, bacteria do get into the meat. Contamination can come from accidents, such as dropping animal parts on the floor. Con-

Careless handling at meat processing plants can introduce bacteria such as Salmonella and E. coli into the food supply.

tamination can occur if meatpackers decide to take shortcuts with safety measures. Sometimes the result is that batches of contaminated meat get into stores or restaurants. The contaminated meat can cause outbreaks of foodborne illness.

CONTAMINATING OTHER ANIMAL PRODUCTS

Eggs can be contaminated with *Salmonella*. This happens when the hen that lays the egg has *Salmonella* bacteria in her ovary. The egg grows in the chicken and picks up the germs.

Milk straight from cows may contain several types of harmful bacteria, including *Listeria*, E. coli, *Campylobacter*, and *Salmonella*. A process called pasteurization can kill the microorganisms in milk. In pasteurization, food producers heat liquids to a temperature just below their boiling point.

The temperature is hot enough to kill most bacteria. All U.S. government agencies involved with food safety urge people never to drink raw milk or eat cheese made from raw milk.

Chickens and their eggs can both be contaminated with Salmonella *bacteria.*

Crops fertilized with manure pose a particular risk for foodborne illness; always wash fruits and vegetables before eating to eliminate any traces of bacteria.

CONTAMINATING FRUITS AND VEGETABLES

Tomatoes, cucumbers, strawberries, and many other fruit and vegetable crops can be contaminated with germs. In Mexico and some countries in Latin America and Asia, farmers often use raw manure as fertilizer. The manure, coming straight from the intestines of cows and other animals, may contain harmful bacteria. The fertilizer helps the crops grow, but it can also contaminate them.

Harmful bacteria might be in the water that farmers use to irrigate fields. Farmers use irrigation systems in regions that don't have enough regular rainfall for crops to grow well. The irrigation water often flows through pipes and sprinklers. But it sometimes flows through ditches in the ground. If the water passes through a cow pasture before it is used for irrigation, the water can pick up harmful bacteria from cow manure. The polluted water could contaminate the crops.

Workers often wash fruits and vegetables after the crop is harvested. But if the wash water is polluted, washing could coat the fruits or vegetables with bacteria.

CONTAMINATING SEAFOOD

Ocean water contains all kinds of microscopic organisms, especially *Vibrio*. Bacteria can build up in sea creatures called bivalve mollusks that take in water while feeding. Clams, oysters, mussels, and scallops belong to this group. They suck in water and filter out tiny particles of food. Suppose *Vibrio* or other bacteria from wastewater polluted with sewage are in the water. The sea creatures will become contaminated. People who eat raw seafood risk getting infected by *Vibrio* and other bacteria.

HUMANS CONTAMINATE FOOD

People sometimes contaminate food they are preparing for others. Kitchen workers in restaurants, hospitals, or school cafeterias can contaminate food with noroviruses. The noroviruses can survive on many kinds of surfaces. An infected person might touch a doorknob, leaving a norovirus behind. The hand of a kitchen worker could pick up the virus by touching the doorknob. The kitchen worker's hand could transfer the norovirus to uncooked meat, vegetables, or other food.

It is usually infected people who contaminate food with the hepatitis A virus. The problem occurs when a

Kitchen workers must handle food safely to prevent the spread of foodborne illnesses.

NOW YOU KNOW

Noroviruses are so powerful that as few as 10 of them in a person's intestines can cause foodborne illness.

person with hepatitis A does not wash his or her hands properly after using the toilet. Touching food with unclean hands contaminates the food. Anyone who eats the food runs the risk of coming down with hepatitis.

Food can be contaminated in homes. The juices of raw chicken, for example, often contain a few *Campylobacter* or *Salmonella* bacteria. Suppose the cook carries the raw chicken on a plate to the barbecue grill. The chicken juices settle on the plate. If the cook puts the cooked chicken back on the same plate, the chicken can become contaminated with the bacteria.

Food left in a warm place can also cause foodborne illness. Bacteria can multiply rapidly in a casserole left on a sunny picnic table. Fish, chicken, and hamburgers can all "go bad" if they are not stored in a refrigerator. But even in a refrigerator, bacteria can grow on food. For example, steak can be refrigerated for three to five days. Refrigerated fish or chicken, however, can spoil after just one or two days.

Bacteria multiply quickly in warm conditions, so refrigerate leftover food promptly after eating.

MORE QUESTIONS THAN ANSWERS IN *SALMONELLA* SCARE

The Monitor
McAllen, Texas
July 20, 2009

A local produce company continued recalling fresh cilantro Monday as investigators tried to figure out who bought the potentially *Salmonella*-tainted salsa staple. ... The U.S. Food and Drug Administration said ... it could not provide a list of what restaurants or retailers might have bought the leafy green ... (or) say how much of the produce had been sold. ... (T)he agency disclosed that a routine test of imported produce uncovered that (the) cilantro could be contaminated with *Salmonella*, a food-borne bacteria that can cause serious and sometimes fatal infections. ... The local produce industry is watching the case closely, but so far does not fear a repeat of last summer when a *Salmonella* outbreak (from) ... jalapeños ... sickened more than a thousand people.

In the spring of 2008, people in New Mexico and Texas began to show up in doctors' offices and emergency rooms complaining of nausea, vomiting, and diarrhea. Suspecting some kind of foodborne illness, doctors ordered lab tests. The tests showed that a strain of *Salmonella* called "Saintpaul" was making the people sick. In most cases, the investigation of an outbreak of foodborne illness leads to a local store or restaurant, and only people in the area get sick from it. In this case, however, more than 1,400 people in 43 states were identified as being infected by the same strain of *Salmonella*.

At first investigators thought the clues pointed to tainted tomatoes as the cause of the illness. But they didn't find the Saintpaul strain in any tomatoes they tested. Tainted tomatoes,

however, could be coming from anywhere. People use fresh tomatoes to make all kinds of dishes, from soup to salsa. To be cautious, officials warned

Salsa contains many ingredients that are often implicated in foodborne illness scares.

everyone in the country not to eat any tomatoes. Further investigation, however, pointed to jalapeño peppers imported from Mexico. These peppers are often mixed with tomatoes in salsa.

DISEASE DETECTIVES GO TO WORK

In tracking down the cause and source of a foodborne illness, investigators are a lot like detectives. They follow a procedure that uses a combination of old-fashioned police work and high-tech tests.

The first step in investigating a foodborne illness is when a doctor reports a case to a local or state health department. A health department investigator interviews the person who became sick. The investigator asks about such things as what the person ate before becoming ill. Did anyone else eat the same thing? Did other people also become ill?

The investigator may come to suspect a particular food, restaurant, or store. Disease detectives may then visit the restaurant or store. They observe how

Investigators visit food processing plants and storage sites to determine the source and scope of contamination.

the food is stored and handled. They pick up food samples and send them to the federal Food and Drug Administration.

CLUES SHOW UP IN THE LAB

The FDA tests the food samples. Lab tests on meat, vegetables, and prepared foods show whether the food is contaminated with a chemical or a microbe.

The goal of state or local health investigators is to match the substance found in the food with the substance found in tests on the sick people. The lab tests might show that there is a virus, bacterium, or parasite in the food. If it is a bacterium, lab workers determine the type, such as *Listeria*, *Salmonella*, or E. coli. Then they want to close in on the exact strain of the bacterium.

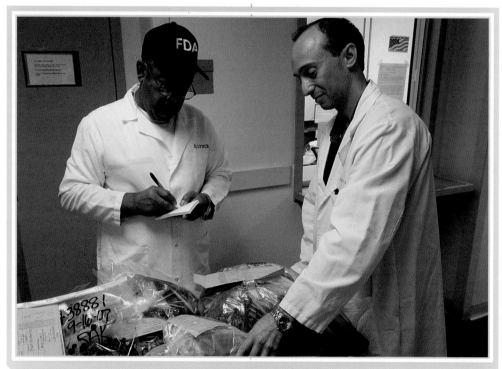

Chemists at the FDA prepare newly arrived food samples for examination and analysis.

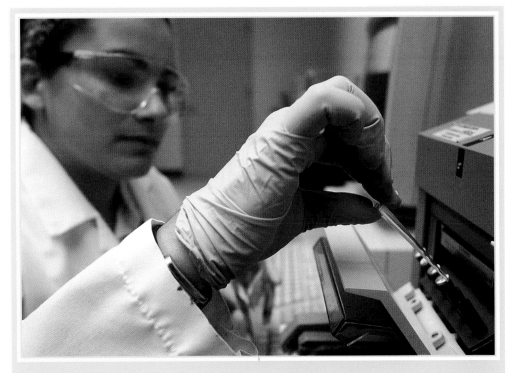

FDA scientists analyze samples of contaminated food to determine the DNA fingerprint of the bacterium causing the outbreak.

To find the strain, investigators can use genetic science. They create a DNA description, called a fingerprint, of the microorganism's genes. DNA is the molecule that genes are made of. Investigators make a DNA fingerprint by running electric current through a gel containing the DNA from a sample. The DNA separates into bands. The pattern of bands shows the organism's unique DNA fingerprint.

Once they have identified the DNA fingerprint, state or local investigators give this information to the Centers for Disease Control and Prevention. The CDC posts it on a Web site. Investigators in health departments all over the United States can see the DNA fingerprints. They can compare DNA fingerprints they find in bacteria infecting people with those on the CDC Web site. In this way, investigators can determine whether the same strain of bacteria is infecting people in more than one place.

FORMING A HYPOTHESIS

To investigate a large outbreak, the disease detectives analyze all the data from interviews and testing. They look for things all the people had in common. After analyzing the data, investigators form a hypothesis, a working idea, about what the source of the outbreak is—a local café, a brand of hamburger patties, cans of tomato sauce, or jalapeño peppers.

Suppose tests show that all the people sickened in one outbreak ate food contaminated with the same strain of E. coli. The people tell the investigators they ate hamburgers grilled at home

before getting sick. All the people bought the raw ground beef from the same chain of grocery stores. That chain buys its meat from one meat-packer. The investigators hypothesize

FDA investigators work to trace an outbreak of foodborne illness back to its source.

that ground beef from that meatpacking plant is contaminated with E. coli.

FINDING THE CULPRIT

Inspectors then visit the plant. They test for bacteria everywhere in the plant, from floors and ceilings to work tables and cutting tools. They test samples of meat being prepared.

Investigators use the same process for suspect fruits or vegetables. They might trace the source of a foodborne infection to a single farm or to a group of farms in a particular area. They send samples to a lab for a DNA fingerprint. The DNA in bacteria found in a meatpacking plant or on farm produce might match the DNA of bacteria from foodborne illness victims. If it does, health departments work to stop the spread of disease.

A government inspector assessed the food safety practices at a lettuce farm in Salinas, California.

SHUTDOWNS AND RECALLS

If the disease detectives trace an outbreak to unsanitary conditions in a single restaurant, they shut the restaurant until the problems are fixed. They might trace the infection source to a single employee, such as a cook infected with hepatitis A. They would then forbid the employee from preparing food until the infection is cured.

If the outbreak comes from food that was sent to several states, the problem is more complicated. Suppose investigators find that contaminated ground beef from one meatpacker was shipped to many stores in other states. Teams of investigators fan out to test meat in these stores. They may have to interview more people who became ill and do more tests. Officials need to be very sure that they have caught the culprit. They must be sure that they have tracked down all the contaminated products. Not only do public health officials shut down plants that produce contaminated foods, but they also recall products from store shelves. Millions of dollars are at stake. The jobs of hundreds of workers could be affected.

< MAD COW DISEASE >

Mad cow disease affects the brain and spinal cord of cattle. Infected cows stagger and sometimes fall down. A strange proteinlike molecule called a prion causes mad cow disease. Researchers first found a similar disease in sheep. In sheep, it is called scrape. The prion can pass to another animal that eats infected brains or spinal cord tissue. Researchers think the cows get the disease by eating animal feed containing the ground-up parts of infected cows—especially brain and spinal matter. Very few people have gotten the disease.

NOROVIRUS OUTBREAK HITS MASS. COLLEGE CAMPUS

The Johns Hopkins News-Letter
April 9, 2009

For 174 people at Babson College in Wellesley, Massachusetts, life has been pretty miserable lately. The norovirus, a bug that causes stomach flu-like bouts of nausea, vomiting and diarrhea, has spread rapidly across the college's campus. ... Norovirus infection typically lasts 24 to 60 hours, and although it is highly unpleasant it is not generally dangerous. The body's own immune system is usually strong enough to take care of the infection on its own, without additional medication. ... The virus ... cannot be cured with antibiotics. ... Those infected with the norovirus are at greater risk for dehydration and can be contagious for up to two weeks. Consequently, the most important key to successful treatment is to keep oneself adequately hydrated.

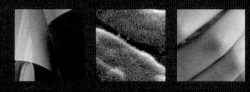

No matter what is causing the food-borne illness, the first step in its treatment is to replace lost body fluids. Vomiting and diarrhea drain away body fluids. The sick person becomes dehydrated. It is very important to keep drinking liquids to replace lost body fluids.

When the symptoms are severe, drinking ordinary liquids is not enough to replace lost fluids. A doctor might prescribe a medicine to drink that does a better job of fighting dehydration. People who are severely dehydrated may need to go to a hospital. There the staff can put fluids

Rest and drinking plenty of liquids are often all the treatment necessary for an attack of foodborne illness.

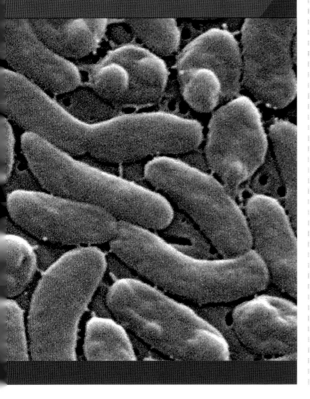

< KILLER CHOLERA >

Severe dehydration can kill cholera victims within a few hours. Cholera is usually caused by drinking water contaminated with *Vibrio* bacteria. Cholera was a serious problem in the United States and Europe until the early 1900s. Good sewers and water treatment plants wiped out the disease in developed nations. Cholera outbreaks still occur in less developed areas of Africa, Asia, and Latin America.

directly into a sick person's bloodstream using a plastic intravenous tube. The fluids contain salts and other minerals that the body needs.

ANTIBIOTICS CAN'T HELP MUCH

Doctors don't usually give antibiotics to people with gastroenteritis. There is no good drug treatment for most E. coli infections. Antibiotics do not help people with *Campylobacter* or *Salmonella* infections get well any faster. Usually the symptoms clear up in a few days. Doctors might, however, give antibiotics to infants, residents of nursing homes, and people with weak immune systems. In such people, the *Salmonella* or *Campylobacter* could more easily spread to the bloodstream.

Doctors also do not prescribe antibiotics if a virus is the cause of a foodborne illness. Antibiotics do not kill viruses. Instead it is important to replace fluids, get plenty of rest, avoid eating while feeling sick, and start with bland foods.

Gastroenteritis caused by para-

Antibiotics are usually not helpful in treating foodborne illness, although in some cases they may be prescribed.

sites, such as *Giardia*, usually clears up in five or six weeks. Doctors can give powerful antibiotics to fight this kind of infection. Pregnant women, however, should not take these drugs. The drugs can cause birth defects in unborn babies.

EMERGENCY TREATMENT FOR POISONS

Illness caused by foodborne toxins, such as botulism, is often a medical emergency requiring treatment in a hospital. Doctors treat poisoning by removing the contents of the stomach. Sometimes they pump the stomach.

Sometimes they give drugs that cause vomiting and diarrhea.

For some poisons, there are drugs called antidotes. For example, doctors can give a patient with botulism a medicine called an antitoxin. This medicine works by keeping the botulin toxin from attaching to nerves. If the botulin toxin has already harmed nerves that control muscles in the lungs, the patient can have trouble breathing. Doctors must hook the patient up to a special machine. The machine, called a ventilator, keeps oxygen moving through the body's airways. The ventilator breathes for the patient. The patient must stay attached to the machine until the antitoxin works.

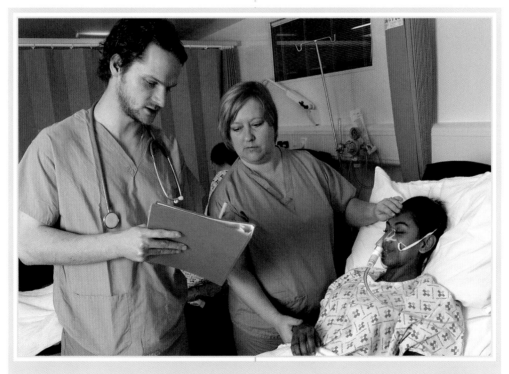

A foodborne illness such as botulism can be serious, requiring hospitalization, intravenous liquids, and assisted breathing with a ventilator.

FOOD SAFETY IN THE AGE OF RECALLS

New York Daily News
July 19, 2009

With 5,000 Americans expected to die and another 75 million expected to get sick this year after eating contaminated food, food safety is a national health concern. ... While consumers are becoming aware of how to cook and store food safely, federal legislation may ensure that government agencies play a more pivotal role in protecting the nation's food. ... The Food Safety Enhancement Act of 2009 would require food companies to conduct hazard analysis programs and to develop written action plans to prevent contamination. Also, the FDA would conduct more frequent inspections of food processing facilities. ... Additionally, the FDA would have the authority to order companies to recall potentially contaminated food. Right now, nearly all recalls are voluntary.

As the saying goes, an ounce of prevention is worth a pound of cure. After terrorist attacks on the United States on September 11, 2001, the FDA set up more rules to protect our food. Today experts think the rule for tracing where imported food comes from should be made stronger yet. This is because once the food is in the United States, more than one company can repack it for sale. They do not have to keep track of where the food goes from there. This seems to be what happened with the jalapeños that caused the *Salmonella* outbreak in 43 states in 2008. The jalapeños were repacked and shipped to many stores and food processors. Because there were no good records tracing the journey of the food, it was hard for

Thorough cooking kills the capsule-shaped Salmonella, *shown magnified 12,000 times by an electron microscope.*

Looking for the source of a 2008 outbreak, the FDA tested tomatoes for Salmonella.

investigators to figure out where the food came from. They sorted through piles of paper sales records, but they didn't have enough information. They thought the tainted jalapeños came from a food producer in Mexico. Mexican officials said this was not so. Some U.S. public health officials believe the mystery of where the *Salmonella* came from may never be solved.

Many levels of laws and rules in the United States are aimed at protecting the food supply and preventing foodborne illness. State and local governments have rules for school cafeterias, restaurants, grocery stores, and food producers. The federal laws are meant to protect the overall national food supply. Some laws involve how farmers grow crops. They limit or forbid the use of dangerous chemicals to kill insect pests or weeds. They call for fertilizers that won't put harmful germs into the soil. They set up rules for meatpacking plants and other places where food is processed.

THE FOOD "POLICE"

Teams of inspectors enforce food safety laws. Some food inspectors work for city or state health departments. Federal inspectors work for the U.S. Department of Agriculture's Food Safety and Inspection Service.

Local health department inspectors investigate the first reports of foodborne illness. They also randomly inspect restaurants. They check the kitchen, refrigerators, and rooms where food is stored. They look for signs of cockroaches, mice, or rats. They watch how food is prepared. If they see conditions that could lead to foodborne illness, they can shut a restaurant down. When the owner corrects the unsafe conditions, inspectors let the restaurant reopen.

Local and state inspectors also visit grocery stores. They check labels on packaged food. Meat, poultry, dairy products, and other food packages must have a "sell by" date. Labels on packaged food must carry other information, such as the ingredients and the name of the company that produced the food.

More than 6,000 federal inspectors work at food processing plants every day. They check the safety of meat and

Food safety inspectors temporarily close restaurants with unsafe conditions or practices.

HEADLINE SCIENCE

eggs produced in the United States. They also work in factories where meat and eggs are used in making other products, such as sausages, frozen dinners, and baked goods.

Federal inspectors help local and state health departments protect food supplies after major disasters, such as hurricanes, floods, and earthquakes. They also check on the safety of food imported from other countries.

PRESERVING FOOD

Since ancient times, people have tried to keep food from spoiling. Long before refrigerators were invented, people learned that salting meat preserves the meat for years. People also pickled foods using salt and vinegar. Salt and vinegar kill bacteria—or at least slow their growth. Since the early 1800s, people have preserved foods by canning. First they boiled the food to kill the bacteria. Then they put the food in jars or cans and tightly sealed them.

Today we have many more ways to preserve food. If food stays cold or

Pickling is a food-preservation process that uses salt and vinegar to slow bacterial growth.

frozen in refrigerators or freezers, it keeps longer. Freeze-drying can rapidly remove water from food, making it much harder for bacteria to grow. One of the newest techniques is irradiation, a process in which radioactive rays are passed through meat or vegetables, killing the bacteria.

HEATING AND COOLING

The ways in which food is cooked and stored are very important in preventing foodborne illness. Thoroughly cooking meat and seafood destroys most microorganisms. Because bacteria can be in the meat used to make ground beef, the temperature inside your burger should reach 160 degrees Fahrenheit (71 degrees Celsius) to kill the bacteria. Federal food agencies urge you to use a food thermometer when cooking burgers or other meats. If you don't have a thermometer, follow the advice of the CDC and don't eat burgers that are red or even pink inside.

Poultry, such as chicken or turkey, should be cooked to at least 165 F (74 C) inside. Steaks and roast beef

Using a food thermometer is the best way to determine whether your food has reached the temperature needed to kill bacteria.

need to reach a minimum temperature of 145 F (63 C). Even leftovers should be heated to 165 F (74 C). The CDC warns people never to eat raw seafood or raw eggs. Thoroughly cooking eggs and seafood kills the bacteria.

Both raw and cooked foods need to be stored at low enough temperatures to slow the growth of bacteria. Keep your refrigerator no warmer than 40 F (4 C). Keep your freezer no warmer than 0 F (minus 18 C). Fresh eggs will keep for up to five weeks in the refrigerator. Steak and pork chops will keep for three to five days in the refrigerator and six to 12 months in the freezer.

Washing your hands thoroughly and regularly is one of the best ways to stop the spread of bacteria.

KEEPING CLEAN

You have probably seen this sign in restrooms: "Employees must wash their hands before returning to work." Hands can pick up and pass along many kinds of germs that cause foodborne illness. Washing your hands with soap and water before handling foods is an important protection.

Wash the counters, tables, and other areas where you are preparing food. Washing cutting boards after each use prevents germs from growing on the surfaces. It is also a good idea to have at least two cutting boards—one only for meats and another just for fruits and vegetables.

And never use the same plate for raw and cooked meat, especially poultry. *Campylobacter* and other bacteria live in the juices of raw poultry. Putting cooked meat on a plate with these raw juices is likely to contaminate the cooked meat.

NOW YOU KNOW

Warm, moist leftovers, such as turkey and dressing, that contain just one bacterium can make you sick. Suppose you leave the leftovers on the kitchen counter overnight. And suppose this single bacterium can reproduce by dividing once every half hour. In the first half hour, one bacterium becomes two. The two bacteria become four, the four become eight, and so on all night long. In 12 hours, that single bacterium's "family" has grown to 17 million new bacteria—enough to make you very sick.

FOUR SIMPLE RULES

The U.S. Food and Drug Administration offers four simple rules to fight foodborne illness in your home:

- Clean: Wash your hands often, along with all the surfaces where you prepare food. Use soap and water, and dry your hands on a clean towel.
- Separate: Keep raw meat away from vegetables to keep germs from passing among them.
- Cook: Heat all food to the right temperature to be sure it gets hot enough to kill germs.
- Chill: Store all foods that can spoil in the refrigerator or freezer; never let such food sit out on kitchen counters.

As anyone who has had a foodborne illness can tell you, it is much better to prevent such illnesses than to treat them. Protecting our food supply is important. But just as important is taking steps to protect the foods in your home from germs that cause foodborne illness. Each family member can help to ensure that food is cooked, handled, and stored safely.

1850
British doctor John Snow, attempting to halt a cholera epidemic in London, becomes the first known person to try disinfecting water with chemicals containing chlorine

1854
Italian scientist Filippo Pacini discovers *Vibrio cholera*, the bacterium that contaminates water supplies and causes cholera

1860s
French scientist Louis Pasteur discovers that bacteria cause food to spoil and that heat kills bacteria

1865
German doctor Theodor Escherich discovers *Escherichia coli*

1884
German scientist Georg Theodor August Gaffky proves that the bacterium *Salmonella typhi* causes typhoid fever, a foodborne and waterborne illness

1886
German chemist Franz Ritter von Soxhlet suggests using pasteurization to make milk safer and longer-lasting

1906
Congress passes the Pure Food and Drug Act

1908
Jersey City, New Jersey, becomes the first U.S. city to use chlorination in public drinking water to kill the bacteria that cause cholera and typhoid fever

1927
The Food, Drug, and Insecticide Administration is created; it is renamed the Food and Drug Administration in 1930

1946
U.S. Centers for Disease Control is founded

1985
In one of the deadliest U.S. outbreaks of foodborne illness, 47 people die after eating cheese contaminated with *Listeria* bacteria

1986
The first case of mad cow disease is identified in the United Kingdom

2003
The first case of mad cow disease in the United States is found in a cow imported from Canada

2008
Milk products tainted with the industrial chemical melamine sicken thousands of babies in China and show up worldwide in products made with Chinese milk

2009
A *Salmonella* outbreak in nine western states prompts the recall of 800,000 pounds (363,000 kilograms) of ground beef that had been processed at a Fresno, California, plant

Timeline

GLOSSARY

antidote
medicine that takes away the bad effects of a poison

bacterium
single-celled microscopic creature that exists everywhere in nature

contagious
spreads easily from person to person or animal to animal

contamination
poisoning or polluting with an impure or unclean substance

dehydration
severe loss of body fluids

gastroenteritis
inflammation of the stomach and intestines that causes nausea, vomiting, diarrhea, and cramps

inflammation
reaction to an infection involving heat, redness, swelling, and pain

intestines
the part of the digestive system through which food moves after passing through the stomach

irradiation
exposure to radioactive rays

irrigation
supplying water to crops through canals, ditches, or pipes

melamine
industrial chemical used to make plastics and fertilizer

microorganism
tiny organism that can only be seen with a microscope

noroviruses
highly contagious group of viruses that cause foodborne illness

parasite
organism that lives off of another organism, giving nothing in return

strain
particular type of bacteria

tainted
contaminated with an unclean or unsafe substance

toxin
poison made by a microorganism or other living thing

virus
bundle of genes in a protein coat that can infect cells

FURTHER RESOURCES

INTERNET SITES

FactHound offers a safe, fun way to find Internet sites related to this book. All of the sites on FactHound have been researched by our staff.

Here's all you do:

Visit *www.facthound.com*

FactHound will fetch the best sites for you!

FURTHER READING

Bjorklund, Ruth. *Food Borne Illnesses*. New York: Marshall Cavendish Benchmark, 2006.

Brands, Danielle A., and Edward I. Alcamo. *Salmonella*. Philadelphia: Chelsea House, 2006.

Coleman, William. *Cholera*. New York: Chelsea House Publications, 2008.

Sherrow, Victoria. *Food Safety*. New York: Chelsea House Publications, 2009.

LOOK FOR OTHER BOOKS IN THIS SERIES:

Climate Crisis: The Science of Global Warming

Collapse!: The Science of Structural Engineering Failures

Cure Quest: The Science of Stem Cell Research

Feel the G's: The Science of Gravity and G-Forces

Goodbye, Gasoline: The Science of Fuel Cells

Great Shakes: The Science of Earthquakes

Invisble Exposure: The Science of Ultraviolet Rays

Nature Interrupted: The Science of Environmental Chain Reactions

Orbiting Eyes: The Science of Artificial Satellites

Out of Control: The Science of Wildfires

Rise of the Thinking Machines: The Science of Robots

Storm Surge: The Science of Hurricanes

SOURCE NOTES

Chapter 1: "India Bans Chocolate Imports From China." *The China Post*. 28 July 2009. 7 Aug. 2009. http://www.chinapost.com.tw/business/asia/india/2009/07/28/218108/India-bans.htm

Chapter 2: "'Norovirus' Cruise Cancelled." Telegraph.co.uk. 8 July 2009. 7 Aug. 2009. www.telegraph.co.uk/travel/travelnews/5772402/Norovirus-cruise-cancelled.html

Chapter 3: Erin Allday. "*Salmonella* Cases Spur Fresno Ground Beef Recall." *The San Francisco Chronicle*. 7 Aug. 2009. 7 Aug. 2009. www.sfgate.com/cgi-bin/article.cgi?f=/c/a/2009/08/07/BUEA19540P.DTL&type=business

Chapter 4: Sean Gaffney. "More Questions Than Answers in *Salmonella* Scare." *The Monitor*. 20 July 2009. 7 Aug. 2009. www.themonitor.com/articles/answers-28707-mcallen-questions.html

Chapter 5: Aleena Lakhanpal. "Norovirus Outbreak Hits Mass. College Campus." *The Johns Hopkins News-Letter*. 9 April 2009. 7 Aug. 2009. http://media.www.jhunewsletter.com/media/storage/paper932/news/2009/04/09/Science/Science.In.The.News.Norovirus.Outbreak.Hits.Mass.College.Campus-3705788.shtml

Chapter 6: Rosemary Black. "Food Safety in the Age of Recalls." *New York Daily News*. 19 July 2009. 7 Aug. 2009. www.nydailynews.com/lifestyle/health/2009/07/20/2009-07-20_food_safety_in_the_age_of_recalls_what_the_government_is_doing_to_protect_us_and.html

ABOUT THE AUTHOR

Darlene R. Stille is a science writer and author of more than 80 books for young people. She grew up in Chicago and attended the University of Illinois, where she discovered her love of writing. She has received numerous awards for her work. She lives and writes in Michigan.

INDEX

antibiotics, 31, 33, 34
antidotes, 35
antitoxins, 35

bacteria, 8, 10–13, 14, 15–16,
  18, 19, 20–21, 22, 23, 27–28,
  29, 33, 40, 41, 42, 43
bivalve mollusks, 21
botulism, 16, 34, 35

Campylobacter bacterium,
  12–13, 19, 22, 33, 43
Centers for Disease Control
  and Prevention (CDC), 12,
  16, 27, 28, 41, 42
chemicals, 4, 5, 6–7, 18, 26, 38
China, 4, 5, 6
cholera, 13, 33
cleaning, 18, 42–43
Clostridium botulinum
  bacterium, 15–16
contagious illnesses, 14, 31
contamination, 4, 6, 8, 9, 10,
  15, 17, 18–19, 20–21, 21–22,
  23, 26, 28–29, 30, 33, 36, 43
cooking, 22, 36, 41–42, 43
Cryptosporidium parasite, 15

deaths, 4, 5–6, 11, 12, 13, 33, 36
dehydration, 13, 31, 32–33
DNA fingerprints, 27–28, 29

eggs, 12, 15, 19, 39, 40, 42
electron microscopes, 14
Escherichia coli (E. coli) bacterium, 11, 12, 14, 15, 18, 19,
  26, 28–29, 33

fertilizers, 5, 20, 38–39
Food and Drug Administra-
  tion (FDA), 23, 26, 36, 37, 43
food processing plants, 17,
  18–19, 28–29, 36, 39
Food Safety and Inspection
  Service, 17, 39

Food Safety Enhancement
  Act, 36
freeze-drying, 40

gastroenteritis, 8, 13, 14, 16,
  33–34
genes, 14, 27
Giardia parasite, 15, 33–34
governments, 6, 18, 19, 36, 38

health departments, 25, 27,
  29, 39, 40
hepatitis A virus, 14, 21–22, 30
hypotheses, 28–29

India, 4
influenza, 14
inspections, 18, 25–26, 29, 36,
  39–40
intestines, 8, 10, 11, 12, 15, 18,
  20, 22
investigations, 6, 17, 23, 24,
  25–26, 26–29, 30, 37–38, 39
irradiation, 40
irrigation, 20

jaundice, 14

labels, 39
lab tests, 24, 26, 29
laws, 38–39
Listeria bacterium, 12, 18,
  19, 26

mad cow disease, 30
manure, 20
Marco Polo (cruise ship), 9
meats, 17, 18–19, 21, 22, 26,
  28–29, 30, 39–40, 41–42, 43
melamine, 4, 5, 6
mercury, 6–7
microorganisms, 7, 8, 10, 14,
  19, 27, 41
microscopes, 7, 10, 14
milk, 4, 5, 6, 19

noroviruses, 9, 14, 21, 22, 31

outbreaks, 8, 9, 11, 12, 14, 17,
  19, 23, 24, 28, 30, 33, 37

parasites, 8, 15, 26, 33–34
pasteurization, 19
PCBs, 7
pesticides, 6, 38
pet food, 6
poisoning, 7, 34–35
pollution, 20, 21
preserved food, 7, 40
prevention, 36, 37, 38, 41,
  42–43
prion molecule, 30

recalls, 4, 6, 17, 23, 30, 36
refrigeration, 22, 39, 40, 42, 43

"Saintpaul" *Salmonella*, 24
Salmonella bacterium, 12–13,
  17, 18, 19, 22, 23, 24, 26, 33,
  37, 38
scrape, 30
seafood, 21, 41, 42
search terms, 6
"sell by" dates, 39
Shigella bacterium, 13
Staphylococcus aureus
  bacterium, 16
storage, 22, 25–26, 36, 39, 41,
  42, 43
symptoms, 7–8, 9, 10, 11, 12,
  13, 14, 15, 24, 32, 33

toxins, 8, 15–16, 34, 35
traveler's diarrhea, 12–13
treatment, 31, 32–33, 34–35

U.S. Department of Agriculture (USDA), 17, 39

vegetables, 10, 20–21, 23–26,
  29, 37–38, 40, 42, 43
ventilators, 35
Vibrio bacterium, 13, 21, 33
viruses, 8, 9, 14, 21, 22, 26,
  31, 33